# Stig Floats in the Moat

By Cameron Macintosh

"It is **so** hot!" said Stig.

"Let's go for a soak, Steff."

"Where can we go?" said Steff.

"We can float in the moat!"
said Stig.

"No! Not in the moat,"
said Steff.
"Dad will not be happy."

"But I'm hot!" moaned Stig.
"I must go in!"

"I will have a wash, too!"
said Stig.

He put lots of soap
in the moat!

The moat filled up with
thick foam!

Then Stig went down
to the moat on a rope.

Stig had lots of fun
in the foam.

"See me float, Steff!"
yelled Stig.

"Oh, Stig!" groaned Steff.
"I hope Dad does not see!"

But then Dad came out!

"Stig!" yelled Dad.
"Get out of that moat!"

"But it's such a hot day, Dad!"
moaned Stig.

'Come with me," said Dad.

Stig got out of the moat
and went with Dad.

"Where are we going?"
said Steff.

Dad led Stig and Steff
to a big red tent.

"You can doze in here,"
said Dad.
"And do not put a toe
in that moat!"

"I like it in here!" said Stig.
"It's **not** hot!"

# CHECKING FOR MEANING

1. How did Stig suggest he and Steff could cool off? *(Literal)*

2. Why did Stig put lots of soap in the moat? *(Literal)*

3. Do you think Dad was really upset with Stig? Why? *(Inferential)*

# EXTENDING VOCABULARY

| | |
|---|---|
| **moaned/ groaned** | What are the meanings of these words? How are they similar in meaning? |
| **foam** | What is *foam*? What did Stig use to make the foam? |
| **doze** | What do you do if you *doze*? Is this a light sleep or a deep sleep? |

# MOVING BEYOND THE TEXT

1. In the past, why did castles have moats? How did people get into the castle?

2. Have you ever had a bubble bath? Why are these bubbles fun?

3. Describe an occasion when you have made bubbles with a bubble pipe.

4. Talk about a time when you did something wrong, but your Mum or Dad didn't get upset with you. Why didn't they?

## SPELLINGS FOR THE LONG /O/ VOWEL SOUND

| o | oa | ow | o_e | oe |
|---|----|----|----|----|

# PRACTICE WORDS

so

go

soak

No

moaned

moat

rope

soap

hope

float

foam

going

doze

groaned

toe